A

BUTTERFLY

IN

GAZA

Poems 2024-2025

A BUTTERFLY IN GAZA

Poems 2024-2025

By Jerry Cimisi

ISBN: 978-0-9999038-6-5
Library of Congress Control Number: 2026905800

"We have forgotten that we have not come to an empty land to inherit it, but we have come to conquer a country from people inhabiting it, that governs it by the virtue of its language and savage culture."
--Moshe Sharett, Israel's second prime minister –

. . . .

DEDICATED TO

The Palestinians of 1948

And the Palestinians of today

Here was a people who mourned
Losses greater than those of their own hearts.

. . . .

It was not thought too unusual during the 1973 war for the army to issue a booklet (with a preface by General Yona Efrati of the central command) written by the central command's rabbi, Abraham Avidan, containing the following key passage: "When our forces encounter civilians during the war or in the course of a pursuit or a raid, the encountered civilians may, and by Halachic standards even must be killed, whenever it cannot be ascertained that they are incapable of hitting us back. Under no circumstances should an Arab be trusted, even if he gives the impression of being civilized."

—Edward W. Said – *The Question of Palestine*

. . . .

Inside this new love, die.
Your way begins on the other side.
–Rumi

FICTION by Jerry Cimisi

THE NEW MAN, A Novel of 9/11

THE PLASTIC ISLANDS, An Eco-Tragedy

WUHAN DREAMS, The Pandemic Begins

CLIMATE, CHANGED, Tales of Ecocide

FORTHCOMING:

ATOMIC Series,
Historical fiction of the Atomic Age

Book One
EINSTEIN'S CHILDREN

Although these poems were written over two years, 82 of the 102 poems were written from the beginning of August 2025 to the end of the year. In fact, 78 of the poems were written from that August to the end of November.

I am never one to hold that quantity indicates quality; I point this out to say the military frenzy with which Israel attacked Gaza City beginning in August 2025 drew an emotional (and I hope literary) rush of poems from me.

Perhaps that assault on Gaza City was the coalescing of all the tragic news since October 2023, now ultimately meeting the most malignant purpose of the occupier; and the previous poems, if speaking enough of tragedy, were the necessary steppingstones to the rush of work that would come from August 2025 onward.

As I write this, Gaza still suffers in the guise of a "ceasefire," as the Palestinians were pressed further into only half of their previous land, then just forty percent, threatening to become a third: a tightened prison in which the occupier is still free to kill, and does so.

Jerry Cimisi
June 2026

Contents

1. In Gaza

A man digs a grave and cries out
To the sky, "Where are you, Arab leaders?"
It's maybe his father's grave, or his.

In the bright hour before a bombed mosque,
In answer a bullet without destination
Sings in this air of sorrow.

In the rain a woman covers her pleading children
With plastic; they crouch quickly within
The thin barriers of her love.

A boy thrusts desperate hands
Into ripped bags of spilled flour
From the aid trucks; this whiteness
Astonishes him; his belly recalls bread.

Stray dogs make their rounds through rubble.
How are they alive, after these months of war?
—The food the soldiers throw at them in mockery,
Or the corpses, legs sticking from debris?

They bark at the soldiers who perform
Their determined duties. Why don't the soldiers
Shoot them? Is there some kinship here?
Acknowledged reflection of creatures caught in madness?

Gravedigger, the devout, mother and children,
Dogs and soldiers—each for that grave
Or another, in the suffering that will outlast.
February 23, 2024

2. Burning Man
(for Aaron Bushnell)

With each step toward the embassy
He had to think of the end
Of his existence: all memory
And being closing swiftly.

He spoke his declaration loudly
By the fenced building; and the fire
Rose sharply around his flesh—with the words
He maintained, in the flames.

In moments pain-made, those words, his cries.
But then, even in that agony
Of last words, an assertion of freedom
Before the burning body fell.

They rushed to him, unprepared,
While an officer tensely pointed a gun
At him—as if the sudden burning man
Was the weapon they all most feared.
March 2, 2024

3. Hind

What's in a child's heart
In the bullet-ridden car
With her dead family,
The bodies that once loved her?
But it's war.

All around her, close and far,
The clash and crash of death,
Drones and coarse soldiers' yells,
Indifferent, yet knowing she's there.

Two men, desperate and brave,
Come racing—after hours, hours—
And then the bullets return.
Does she—do they—die quickly?

Are there depths of dying, of loss,
Pains of the body and spirit,
Past the closing terrors of Earth,
Freed finally from our horrors?
But it's war.

May 4, 2024

4. Burning Hand

You sleep in a tent outside the hospital
And the bombs and guns and drones
Come often. But you're used to that.
Then silence. It holds you, sleep returns.

And then the bomb and the fire happen at once—
The sound and the flame. And the flame
Is your body. No words for this pain.

But then it passes, shreds your senses
And your arm rises up from the bed,
Weightless in its destruction,
Suspended silhouette in the flames.

It's not agony, it's not farewell.
Your body too ravaged to move—
Your hand the sign of a language you never knew.

October 14, 2024

5. *Funerals*

Children standing by the graves of parents,
Parents standing by the graves of children.
And here a child sleeping between
The graves of his parents;
And there, parents grasping the dirt
Of their child's grave.

Or a funeral for just a head,
All that's left, carefully wrapt,
All that's left of the whole.
Funerals for body parts
Named by shredded clothes,
Dead limbs jumbled in earth.

But is it earth-like this rubble,
No life here, only dust?
Forever the shredded flesh
Scattered in this violated earth
Is paused within us: what seeds
Do flesh and bone and blood become?

November 19, 2024

6. *Kamal Adwan Hospital*

It's easy to point to the evil
The days of strewn flesh have shown;
But this is marker to all the deaths before:
The infant in the ravaged hospital,
The oxygen supply destroyed, perhaps parents
Also gone into the rubble of the bombs.
So short a calendar of life, bereft of breath….
The push of lungs to grasp what it cannot….
What thought, thoughts we cannot know,
What thought sears through the small limbs
And soul as it takes last moments in this world?
Stunned and doomed, we know this evil.

November 22, 2024

7. *The Dogs of Netzarim*

In the strip cut across Gaza
The dogs eat bodies snipers provide.
Amidst war food is scarce for the outcast,
So every hunger welcomes flesh.
From their distance the soldiers smile
At beasts pulling muscle from bone.
Phones flash photos of this repast,
A captured family feast,
Frequently arranged—
From the sea to the occupier's land.

December 20, 2024

8. Frozen Babies

Life is warm. In the tents it's cold.
She awoke twice in the night, crying,
Said the father. In the morning—
The frozen child was wrapt in white.
What prayers offered up in that dawn
—Bitter, grey and yellow—
Amongst these redundant crimes?
It was not the first child
Whose infant dreams were frozen
In the dark of drones and bombs.
—And the memory the mother takes
Is the warmth of the night before,
The name she cooed at the life of her womb.

January 11, 2025

9. Ceasefire

Of course, so many I loved
And the places they filled gone,
He said. *I waited in fear and pain*
And mourning for this to end.
Now I'm released to hope.
But I don't know hope.
Left with only memory and rubble,
Is there meaning now, to go beyond,
Past today? In the midst of celebration

His hands made a sad movement
As if caressing something that had been taken
And would never sleep with him again.
January 15, 2025

10. Returning Home

The building she had lived in
Had had three floors. It still stood,
Except for the walls the bombs
Had ripped away. It was a skeleton
With a flap of skin here and there
Hanging on to a part of its life.
The woman climbed the wreck of her home
And from a window blasted free of glass
Looked from that top floor height
At the other ruins of her people
And the others who had returned,
The dispossessed, entering ravaged doorways.
Birds flew past her. She felt the beat of wings,
Creatures unweighted by armies;
Shook her head at their cries. She considered
She shared their height, and they too
Shared the vision of those unwinged
Below, moving through the leftover dust of war.
January 20, 2025

11. Finding Bodies

They tried to be systematic
But the fragments of destruction
(Something so vast now)
Jumbled their progress—metaphor
For the disarray of the dead.
Some were more bone than flesh by now,
As if the truth of the body had emerged
With violence, and fell into sections when raised
To the light—and the recognition of the living.
And then some bodies, like rare apparitions,
Appeared complete, revealed in borderwork
Of debris, a final frame for battered life.
I knew that one, a man said. *In the market*
He sold— But the memory of what the dead sold
Was lost in the recognition of the weight
Of this body added to the others—
To which, as final voice, might be added names.

January 22, 2025

12. The Prisoner

I watched the gaunt Palestinian man
On the video speak slowly about prison,
His face grey, as if sunlight had permanently left him.
They tortured us day and night.
It would have been more merciful
To kill us. His pained face spoke of beatings,
Little food. *We ate every other day*
So the children could eat. We were older,
We could resist hunger.
Memories of what the universe had allowed.
I was left most with that: the children
Penned in with beatings, near starvation.
How much can any life resist,
Until collapse? What happens to the torturers
When there are no bodies, none, nothing
Save the accounts of their deeds?

January 26, 2025

13. After the Dictator

I began numbering the days
Of the dictatorship. As if
A new calendar, marking another A.D.
But it began before that first marking.
When? The children I saw burned in Gaza?
No. The West marking out the sands for oil?
No. The faiths that have broiled the Earth,
Proclaiming cruelties bound to the covenants
Of the gods they formed, intuiting the mirrors
They did not yet have? I fear
We became thus simply being human.
Our only freedom from each new dictator
Is to leave the primal human in lost ages
In some arcane hall of fallen species.

February 16, 2025

14. The Star Naming People

The occupiers cut the electric
And in the dark where winter still held,
The stars were hard, as if
Just to see them was cruel.

But then someone said our people named them.
It was the Arabs who said: *Rigel*
And Betelgeuse and Aldebaran—
The names of so many star jewels.

And the besieged looked up then,
In sudden loving, pride and power.
As if even the occupiers knew
They had to accept a heaven older

Than their rule—what every weapon
Could not, through all these years, efface.
No star naming people could ever be swept
From earthly night among these worlds.

March 16, 2025

15. Diagnosis

The parents, grimed with bomb blasts,
Brought their dead child to the hospital.
The doctor looked down at the shattered head.
His expression had long ago gone beyond horror.
The father was silent; the mother's voice
Came from another place—a place
That wouldn't recognize the war: *What can you do?*
The worn doctor tried to speak, could not.
His body shook a little, with exhaustion
And despair. No one noticed.
From some distance in the ravaged hospital
Were sharp cries of other flesh.
The dying, the almost dying, who tried
To escape from the prison of a bed.
At last the doctor said, *She can rest here.*
He feared the delusion he spoke
For a child severed from the grace of respite.
He feared the parents who weren't screaming.
He heard their breathing; he took it into his blood.
In a long silence they all stood by the girl.
Beyond were the bombs, further diagnosis.

April 12, 2025

16. Gaza, June 2025

By now the killing is so constant
One is past considerations of evil.
This is effect and cause beyond unravelling.
You can't grasp what thunders down here.

This horror is life; each day the chance
Of not living. You're pushed out onto a borderland
Of twilights. One pauses before the bodies—
Shredded, rent—like a common task of grief
That will not end. Grief, precarious life—
And the hot sun, or the cold, on the debris,
Seeped into every former form
Of the abstract rubble, cities rearranged
By the signals of destruction.
Are you chosen to witness this—or change it?

And then, suddenly, one sees a child,
Walking in the light, unharmed,
A voice talking to the self that still lives,
Eyes grasping something beyond the world
You keep seeing—and you are struck
By what may yet come to the blood of the future.

June 2, 2025

17. Street Dreams in Gaza

In some still corner of the street
A girl, seven or eight, sleeps facedown
By a building worn with war,
Its wall a mosaic of bullets and weather.
Up the street men mill and murmur,
Their bodies caught in tense survival.

Her child's form of dirty clothes sprawled in exhaustion,
Her pillow the hard concrete not yet rubble.
Faceless to us, does she dream
Of the now dead brother, playing
Beneath another sky, of the father
Carelessly shot, carrying a sack of flour?
Of the ravaged ragged family, moving and moving,
Fleeing again, the bombs, the drones,
Overwhelming every flight?

Or perhaps she does not dream at all.
Violence and exhaustion drowning all dreams,
She can only awake bitter and stunned,
Eyes blinking, breathing sadly,
And wish again for that facedown sleep
On the hard, inhuman world.
—And return to the men
Who cannot protect her.

June 4, 2025

18. I Want To Know What the Donkey Thinks

I want to know what the donkey thinks
Who pulls the cart with the wounded and dead
To the hospitals and graves of Gaza.

Moving with its weary strength,
Head not even turned to the sorrows
Of its burdens, ordered to pull bodies,
Again and again across bombed streets.

We too are beasts chained to paths of madness
Looking ahead, while the murdered sap our strength.
If only we could reach the place where the final bodies
Are taken from us, and we are not needed to return
And we can look back, to see life, and light.

I want to know what the donkey thinks
Who pulls the dead. Is there any philosophy
That makes it go on, any hope?

July 1, 2025

19. Kites

The children made kites from the worn fabrics of war,
Stretched them against splinters from doors
And beds, and with the treasures of string
Tethered them from the rubble to the sky—

Small hands holding creations they imagined
Flew even above the bombs, every shudder
Of wind and unsteady hands the tremor of freedom,
This thin line linking them to heaven.

They could keep this peace for an hour,
No destruction touching their kites and pleasure,
Their hearts falling into the sky of that faith
That makes these moments of children immortal.

July 5, 2025

20. Toys

The child held a stuffed toy in the rubble of Gaza—
Some battered animal, companion to the hands
That have lost so much. Was it his, carried
With instinct and fear through the evacuations?
Named when new, name remaining through being worn?
Or had he just come upon it in the destruction,
Another child's companion, some bomb-blasted orphan
Who has lost both childhood and parents?
And perhaps afraid to name what another had?
And the rubble—is it this boy's home
Or another devastated mirror of all homes lost,
Destroyed like the toys of children, only here
And there retrieved in the stunned numbness
Of war without end? Homes, toys, children:
Every one each prey to the genocide
Whose history unravels now, in light and night,
But whose armies deny is written in their tongue.

July 9, 2025

21. The Lost Aid Seekers

He left the day before yesterday, said the old woman,
My son. To get food. His family was killed.
She closed her eyes as if seeing the murders,
Corpses weighted on eyelids
We were the only ones left. The wind blew sand.
The day before yesterday, she said, blinking.
The husband mouthed: *A week.*
There was a pause; as if days or a week
Fell into the same hell of time.
The old woman looked into the heated horizon.
He said, most of them come back.
The old man nodded, grunted: *"Food."*
But he spoke it like pronouncing a bitter folly.
No one knows, she said. *So many....*
She lost words and thought—too much truth.
Her husband wiped at his eyes,
Breathed in resolution with a sniffle.
His wife nodded. *We're still hungry. Nothing to—*
Words lost again. Then: *My son left before yesterday.*
The old man said, aloud, clearly now, *A week.*
Then both were silent, waiting.

August 4, 2025

22. Blood on the Streets

Somewhere there is always blood on a street
In Gaza. Bright, of course, and terrible
When it's spilled…and then of the texture
Of surfaces. Hours after the body is taken
To hospital or grave or hospital then grave,
Others walk by the mark of murder,
Abstract signs suddenly given,
And step alongside its now darkened borders:
You can't disrespect the borders
Of the fallen. So many maps
Of reddened, browned territories these months,
These years; and sun will bake the blood
And rain thin it, and night almost hide it—
Though often the moon will cast a last sheen
On something once so much in the instant of life,
Make it apart from the ruins.
Thus the streets of Gaza: blood bright,
Blood waning to somber—cartography that binds
The hours and dreams of those who yet
Hold their blood in flesh, in the knowing
A moment comes when they might add
To the street map of the fallen.

August 12, 2025

23. The Girl Over Her Mother's Grave

Some poems don't quite get written
But they stay in fragments that insist.
More than a year ago now, I saw
A girl, maybe six or so, sobbing
Over her mother's grave, her hands
Clutched in the sand. So close below
That earth was the woman from whom
The girl had come; the girl of the flesh
Of the woman below. My words then
And not really now ever right enough
To honor the buried body and the girl
Wracked with the loss murder so freely gave.
But I have to note it, and tell you,
And carry it through days and years,
And search for future words—
So when I see again the mirror of this
I will speak a declaration so sharp
It will pierce the complacency of killers
Blinding them and us
With a sorrow too definite to allow forgiving
From those who saw.

August 12, 2025

24. Weather

The weather became the enemy too:
The cold, the cold rains that made the face raw,
The heat, that made the body a weight,
The humid rains that pooled in mud
And gave ugly reflections of sky.
Both rains flooded the tents.
And sudden winds that could unravel
The heart, like the battering of the bombs.
Inside the blood was whipped,
Like shards of torn clothes.
There were times, separate times,
When man or woman or child
Stood in this hostility of weather
And stolidly accepted it—not a surrender,
But as if stepping alongside
The agony of elements by chance given,
And breathed in the slow fact of existence,
The slow suffering of time the weather
Used as weapon, undirected but ensnaring,
And always redundant,
As if additional ally of murderers.

August 16, 2025

25. Evacuation

Saw this on a video, if just for a moment:
An old woman in heavy dirty black
Trying to evacuate, bent over
So much her hands too were legs:
On all desperate fours, hands scraping
Over the dirt as she fled
To some distant moment's safety.
—And then she was gone.
There was just some empty space
Of the land of war, an indifferent sky.
The end of her days had become
No memory of the child who could have run
Here in happiness. This terrible passage
Only here for my eye, who did not know her.

August 16, 2025

26. *Superman*

And suddenly—but so quietly—a boy
With a Superman cape and costume
Walks down the bombed out streets,
The shattered homes with broken windows.
He has that soft smile children have
Caught in some instinctive, private play.
He barely notes a stain of blood on the rubble
He passes; it's like some rock in a terrain
That's common and doesn't threaten.
The adults point. Some laugh softly. Some feel
The guts of fear when you understand the self
Abruptly. He's a child, they can say, taking himself
From the horror here, the threat he'll die
Like the other children taken from their future
In the white shrouds an aid truck just brought.
But some at least comprehend they too
Walk these streets with the costume of some myth
The bombs can cruelly end. One needs
The mark of fantasy to live,
The vision of native powers,
A last honor, one's own.

August 18, 2025

27. *Lies of Goodness*

The starving can tell no lies with reaching lips,
While you, Trump and Netanyahu, feed ten times
On what those you starve need a fraction.
Your lips of course are full of lies,
The lies of goodness, of consecration:
Great America Again, Greater Israel, the titles
Of the history you lay down with the vile delusion
You insist—smiling, demanding—we share.
Your enemies swept away, openly or secretly,
The wasting bodies here, their weight approaching
Ineffable air, eyes closing—without memory, you hope.
You don't want memory, you don't want
The abducted opposition, the one who shouts for freedom
Leaving any impress you can't brush from your suit.
But no land is swept of those who passed and suffered.
The blood is not dried to nothing in the sun;
Blood is not washed by rain from rubble.
The hopes and songs and days and loves
Of the history that lived before you
And alongside you—it's never gone.
You Christian Zionists, you Jewish Zionists,
Your God that chooses you; your prayers
In Congress and at the Wall: history,
And perhaps even tomorrow, makes all disguise
Fall away: your lies of goodness. The flesh
And those whom you called enemies,
The children of your enemies,
All starved and battered from your crimes:

The fact they needed to be killed
Takes all goodness from your lies.
And it will be known. And acknowledged.
And you will be forever marked by the true costume
Of every deed you told us was a different act.
We saw. We see. We damn you with our eyes.
You cannot, you can never, lie to our vision.

August 22, 2025

28. *You Can Die of Grief in Gaza*

You don't have to be shot or bombed—
You can die of grief in Gaza.
Seeing your mother's face collapse in the frame
Of her hijab, mouth crooked with death;
The man passing you do not know
Grasped to his chest the white shrouded child
You can never know now;
The violated outline of apartments ripped down to rubble,
Shards of floors precarious against sky
With shattered, light twisting windows;
One tower of a mosque left risen in broken streets
And alongside men bent down on prayer mats,
Their faces to the fabric that covers destruction;
And wandering to the shoreline as if the seas
Pull you to freedom, the young diving and soaking
Themselves in the heat, moments of relief,
Young skin shining with the ancient sea,
Playful on the hard edge of apocalypse—
Oh, every vision gives grief; and when
The hungry stagger by, their eyes flamed in bone,
The moving angles of skeleton in their clothes….
The weight overwhelms. You want a room
Whose windows don't see this, and a sky
Where sudden bombs don't scream and fall
And shred the tents like the wings of birds
In demonic arson. –To rest, the eyes closed
To the simpler death of grief.

August 23, 2025

29. *Olive Trees*

It was always painful when he remembered as a child
His father raging and crying as the occupiers
Destroyed the olive trees. He remembered looking
To the glistening oil in the glass bottle in the kitchen,
As if that surface of oil and glass reflected
The tears and anger that wracked his father.
Those trees were here before the Nakba,
Shouted his father, *My grandfather—*
But the child submerged the lineage of cultivation
In his own fears at his father's fear and sorrow,
As his mother looked upon her husband
Without an expression in a manner worse than pity.

Older, the trees were his. That morning,
That long day when the soldiers came
With bulldozers, and droning saws
And the trees, a hundred years old,
Were sawed without mercy,
Were uprooted to tender roots—
How something so venerable could be
So vulnerable—and he shouted, as his father
Might cry out…and the soldiers pointed their guns—
And laughed. He retreated, trembling,
Anger a current crashing in his blood.
Inside he said to his own children, "I will kill them."
He'd lived through months and months of genocide;
But this seemed the last wound,
Its only answer to return death to the killers themselves.

The face of his wife recalled his mother's;
He broke into weeping, at every horrible choice.
He wanted desperately to fulfill his vow.
August 24, 2025

30. Death Is Hungry

Fewer and fewer children talked about peace and returning
To their homes, to school. They spoke
Of food, of death, of their families in Jannah.
Food and death live together in the heart
When one is absent and the other alongside
Every hungry breath. One bony child,
Whose face edged through the flesh
Held a battered metal dish smeared
With not enough food and squatted
In a paint-peeling corner and ate slowly,
In the most somber way, as if to eat
Were a difficult act—and then slowly looked up
At someone who inquired if he needed more
And responded with a young voice made old,
And said, *There's always something you eat*
That is the last thing you eat. Then his voice
Trailed into mumbled memory of a friend
Who last ate lentils—before he starved,
Days later, that last meal apparently
A diversion on the route to emaciation
And death. The living child put down
The battered dish and said, *I'm not hungry now.*

Perhaps this meal was also too difficult
A diversion upon the path he'd be thrust.
He's peaceful now, he said of the dead friend.
It was the most quiet envy, and it hung in the air.

August 27, 2025

31. The Camera

The camera had blood on the thick cannister
Of the lens—and dirt and dust from the rubble
Of the bombs. One of the journalists still living
Held it as if an offering to herself—and others.
So much vision had come through this tool
Of telling the horror. She looked through it now,
Scanned her companions, surviving these days,
These weeks, these months, these years.
Their faces understand they too were marked,
And might be blown apart without leaving
An instrument. How the bearers of cameras
Understand martyrdom—not simply as the dead,
But their sacrifice for the stories of the dead.
They were all marked here: the tellers of their people,
The people who trudged to some lie of safety.
And here, the battered camera, construct
Of vision that no lies could betray—
The bodies who had come into its vision
Not gone, but legacy.

August 30, 2025

32. *In the Rubble*

They dug through the bright dust rubble
With bare hands, hands that quickly bled
And were whitened too by the dust:
Red-white flesh grasping an arm—the edge
Of the mystery: if the body yet lived—
The point of the slow extraction
Of form that had moved seconds ago.
Over and over again, all these days,
They cleared the rubble, found bodies
Living or dead, or battered into the between place
In which all of life seemed now. Their own bodies battered,
They brought the sadly resurrected
To ravaged hospitals with wounded doctors
And returned to other tragedies, duplicate crimes
They could not solve, but only occasionally
Lessen, as if teased with a victory
Now and then, but which the next extracted
Dead man or woman or child mocked them—
Endless involuntary victims crushed
In the cascade of the evil of the bombs.

September 1, 2025

33. Portraits

Still life faces on the streets of Gaza:
Portraits of the dead—battered faces,
Or some hardly streaked with blood;
Some die with eyes open; as if sight
Could never have expected any ending at all.
We have illusions of last moments
Held pitifully like a photograph;
But we peer close and just see reflections,
The observer still moving in the days they've left.
Others have their eyes closed, shut
Against all the world, as if ashamed
Of being brought into the madness
That absurdly brought this end.
Some lie on their backs, some on their sides:
It's a position of chance among the chance
Of their deaths…. All have become
Horizontal signposts of the passage here:
Entire bodies like faces unmasked
By all the crimes they have suffered.

September 3, 2025

34. *Observer and Victim*

He stopped to watch the bombs blocks away
Shatter buildings, the explosions reaching him
With fine ash. He hadn't paused there
To be on the border of safety;
He was too exhausted to flee further;
His legs barely held him, his arms shook,
Could grasp nothing, lift nothing.
He swayed with the exhaustion of being trapped.
And watched the buildings fall, collapse,
A thick black cloud folded into a face arsisen,
Thinking of the lives who once teemed there,
Buildings empty now— Or, he imagined at once
(And started in fear) someone left, as exhausted as he was,
The battered body deciding it could no longer flee,
That the best escape was annihilation.
This shocked him with the truth of a vision.
He sunk down to the rubbled street,
Awaiting the approaching strike,
When his own ash would settle finely
On the streets just beyond where he once stood.

September 5, 2025

35. *Stolen Graves*

The child's father had been killed a year ago.
In the summer heat a more fiery thing
Tore down from the sky and left a limp body
Streaked with blood on the hard street.
The earth he was buried in was softer.

There was a frail, pale stone—but it was lovely.
With a photo etched in careful art.
The mother took the girl often to the grave
Of the man who only calendars ago had been
A child too. And this living child spoke
To her baba with the habit that had turned
Tragedy into comforting habit. She was
One child among a nation of murdered fathers.

But today the mother at last called her away
With a sorrow the girl did not have—but
Could she sense it? The bombs weren't far;
And the mother knew the grave too would be taken.
Still the child left her baba's place almost cooing:
A ritual safe in memory. Which she would need.

Even the graves were not to be left.
The murder would not be complete
Unless even the murdered past was done.
The girl did turn back once—almost a puzzled glance,
Birth to something memory would explain.

September 5, 2025

36. Housewares

They fled their homes before the bombing,
Returned in the settled indifferent dust to salvage
What they could: blankets, clothes, the luxury of a toy,
Before the exhausting flight south.
But how much could they carry? They sold the rest
To the man in the patched tent weighted against wind
With genocide goods, paying them in hard coin
Or Bitcoin, worn paper money for food
And fuel bribe-smuggled from Egypt—and left
Feeling the absence of what they could not grasp,
Danger keeping them from looking at the things of life
That could be no longer kept. –While the buyer
Knew in advance his own loss: whatever he could
Sell of what had been sold to him, there would remain
This jumble of a household of his people
When he in turn could not be kept by profit
To remain. His own flight would be the abandonment
Of a museum of the Everyday…and he would turn
At least once to honor it, he promised himself,
Like the farewell, haunted gaze in a myth,
As the things of this world, pillows and cups
And a stool for a child became flame and ash.
What several things would he take for his own flight?
He didn't know. Perhaps it would be a final freedom,
This surrender to violation and flight, without
Anything save his body, to a future
In which any mercy seemed wholly unknown.

September 6, 2025

37. Geography

He found some height on some rubble
And quietly swept his eyes about the landscape
Torn from structure, the grey jumble that led to a horizon
That lined the edge of devastation with the sky.

This was always a sad vision; well,
Those would be his first thoughts:
Replaying the bombs, explosions of flame
And smoke, the screams of survivors
Fleeing what was sudden, yet expected.

Then he went beyond sadness.
Not resignation, not acceptance,
But sitting with something beyond
—No, apart—from destruction.
Here was the world, everything was settled:
Final. He had no questions;

He had no weight of tragedy.
Despair was something he had shed.
It was as if…he didn't have the words for it,
But it was something in the nature
Of now moving past all lies. Nothing
Had saved this land. The survivors too
Had shed it; their bodies were the land,

Moving where the land was not—
As if they stepped within new places

The destroyers could never envision.
Each living soul that remained
Was the resistance of a geography
Even their cities had to fall from.
They brought a land with them—him too—
That touched the horizon more viscerally than rubble.
September 9, 2025

38. Scavengers

The two girls, maybe five or six, had found food
In the black garbage bags hot in the sun.
They ate quietly, too young to know
Why they had been starved. After all,
They could hardly remember times without war.
Life had narrowed them; they moved through it.
Adults nearby looked sadly at them:
At least the children had found food.
Nearby flies buzzed by other black bags:
Another signal that had become common.
After the finishing, the girls went toward the flies—
Who gave way angrily; but here the children
Found something that was even beyond
Their hunger. They paused; it could not be said
Their faces were even sad. They moved off, in silence,
In a submission to the needs that yet held them.
September 10, 2025

39. The Lights Above

The electricity was cut and the Strip was dark
Doom in the night; soon the occupiers
Let the fire bombs drop—slowly, it seemed—
Through the thick sky: to give sight
For more killing. They had taken hope
From illumination. There was a fate
In those descending, approaching constellations;
And the eye held it all a moment,
Alongside the fear. Then the land was bright
With burning and the true bombs came
And the eyes that had been upward
Were the seeing of the bodies
That could flee only across the land,
Dogged vision fixed ahead.
They could not ascend to where the fire
Had formed and decreed its herald to them.

September 11, 2025

40. The Tent of My Relatives

(The witnesses write these poems.)

We used this tent for two years; we can't use it anymore.
We went to the tent of my relatives; it was too small.
I had my wife, our children, my mother. Too small.
They told us to come here to Al-Mawasi, we'd be safe,
There would be shelter and water—
And we would not be killed.
It was a lie. The occupation always lies. Everything they say.
I have no money for a new tent. We struggle with hunger.
My nephew is only thirteen. I can't send him for food.
They are still shooting everyone at the aid sites.
He will die. They won't protect children.
I think they want to kill children.
They want to make sure we are not here tomorrow.
I tell people why move, why leave, they kill everywhere.
Why not just die here, on the land, in the city?
We know these places. Better to die
Where you know where you are.
If the last walls we have are tents
We have the sky and the earth.
The occupation cannot take the sky and the earth.
There are things even they can't kill.

September 13, 2025

41. The Witnesses Write the Poems II

They destroy the city block by block
They gave us only enough warning to run outside.
I saw the bomb come down, in the sky,
Saw it hit the building—every apartment.
Like eyes blown out of an animal.
I knew those people: they are out here,
Like us now—some are not out in time.
The building buries them. Their rooms
Are their graves. We have nothing, there is nothing.
I don't have a pillow, I don't have a blanket
For my children. Yesterday I heard children
A block away, screaming; Everything come down on them.
Block by block, everything comes down,
Soon there will be no city, only the memory
Of one. And when we are all dead,
Who will remember?
No one can tell the truth of a city that has gone.
The killers will say it's desert, like when they came here—
And lied about the cities they took from us.

September 13, 2025

42. *I've Seen the Pietà a Thousand Times In Gaza*

I've seen the Pietà a thousand times in Gaza,
The mothers darkly enrobed, wrenched
Into private catastrophe, bent and cradling
Their dead child, who had moved moments ago;
The fathers, bloodied, bare armed and stiff,
Legs stuck in the street, looking ahead
At landscapes of madness, holding a dead son
Across their chest, a still warm shield of sorrow.
And children, themselves ravaged by bombs,
Comforting themselves with dead siblings,
Clutched as if the force of their embrace
Could erase all and every violation,
Not allowing this shattered link of family.
I've seen the Pietà a thousand times in Gaza,
As evil comes to all the blood of this land;
And those who hold the dead bear a grief
That will be resurrected every day of their lives.

September 14, 2025

43. A Child Still Smiles in Gaza

In some pause in the bombing and flight,
A mother played a game of hide and appear
Between the tents. The boy could not have been
More than year, birthed in genocide, but here
A smiling face, as if safe, crawling between tents
And laughing at his mother's sudden face and voice.
It was a joy for both, timeless, and as if
Some portal of the reality that should be
Had captured them with entrance.
Then the mother had a stab of worry
And gathered the child, went into the tent.
The boy still giggled, now with tired pleasure.
But his mother did not want that treasured moment
Severed by the bombs. They would come, perhaps
Not for hours, but they would come.
Resigned with her own exhaustions the mother
Forced her imagination to secure a future
For her child: of laughter in a legendary land
Whose tents were not worn with war.
And when the bombs did come, the child
Look puzzled, cried a little, then slept, whimpering,
Stored in his soul the danger of the only life
He had known, and his mother's vision,
Cast so tremulously forward. And in that sleep
His smile did return, like the assertion his mother craved.

September 16, 2025

44. *The Calls of Gaza*

Like a thousand others the woman ran
To the building just bombed, calling out
The names of her family. It was a height of rubble,
The cruelest transformation,
And she touched this immovable weight,
Jabbed hands into cracks of darkness
And kept calling the names—the despairing
Call to prayer that is the call of these days,
These calls the echoes of Gaza—as if the sounds
Could return the dead, batter death
Into surrender, into life's return.
The horror hadn't fully grasped her,
But it was settling in, deeper,
And she continued the names, asserting
Her blood, their blood: *They're in there!*
She implored to no one now, just statement
Of her whole life: outside, alive, stricken,
The living victim by the tomb of her dead.

September 18, 2025

45. A Son, Come Home

He left with his son for the aid;
The sun had just cracked the sky
As the shore brought in a chill from the sea.
Hours later, not fully returned, the sun blasting.
He walked weighted in a wasteland
So thoroughly bombed its land
Seemed the desert of destroyed civilizations,
Powder and fragments making grey his legs—
Weighted with the dead, white shrouded body
Of his son. There were no questions to ask,
No words when life snaps your soul to splinters.
He looked ahead or down, his eyes not seeing,
Seeing no land or others, the weight of his child
The burden of the elements. Cruelty,
Evil, had become elemental here…
And he remembered the chill off the waters
At dawn: the horror that he could not return
To that hour of his child's life.
The sun could not lift this impress
Off his soul now, certainly not his flesh.
He kept walking, thinking of no destination.

September 18, 2025

46. Dystopia

You can't believe you're seeing this caravan in your lifetime:
This must be an old history, or the apocalypse promised.
The things of their lives packed on cars and trucks
To impossible heights, or roped on carts pulled
By exhausted donkeys—or on the backs of men,
As exhausted as the beasts. A weighted, bent,
Furious man with a pot on his head
That should have made him ridiculous,
But his fury and his cry and the blaze
Of his sun bronzed face gave him honor.
These are the tears of a man! he cried out.
I cannot stand, I can't move! But he moves on,
Grasping the pot as it falls from his head in exclamation.
Somewhere else in this line of exodus, a woman,
Black shawled, face older with these years,
Had her own cries at the void:
Can't everyone see! Why can this happen!
And somewhere, politicians give calm
Lying explanations. *It is sadly necessary....*
And there, after a bombing, paramedics
Find a child by a waving hand,
Stuck out of the rubble—and nearby,
A child not alive, in death's full exhaustion,
And right by that another child,
So obliterated and charred, and lifted
As if some long stretch of flesh and bone
And honored with a white shroud,
The shrounds that are everyday equipment here,

Flags not so much of surrender in this exodus
But incessant markers of the absurd.
For what else is this but the absurd
To which all the calm lies led, the history lessons
That hide with their history this day and hour.
September 18, 2025

47. The Mahagony Man

Stripped to the waist, bone and brown,
A man older than Israel and who now
Seemed marker of old Palestine,
Of a thousand years of sun and weather,
Man of frail dark wood, crosslegged
On a dirty blanket, the skeleton and skin
The finished flesh of the weeks of starvation.
His eyes blinked at the displaced around him,
Moved his head a little at a darting fly
As if in some sort of venerable recognition;
Once he sucked in his stomach;
—You could see the starved muscles stuck to the spine—
And exhaled with the softest sigh.
But there was mostly silence and stillness
From this man who had been battered
By every year of cruelty and this year's crescendo.

A girl becoming woman came to him and said,
We have some food, grandfather. She spoke
To the withered past that had survived.
He was probably father to her grandfather.
He looked up at her with a sort of wonder.
Food was a miracle now. And then his look
Was kindness: as if her existence offered
Him the greatest sustenance. His arms
Floated up, grasped her hand in two hands.
He smiled and mumbled. What did those old hands
Feel like to the young? The smile she returned
Was one of relief. Perhaps she'd been worried
He was too far gone in the ascetics of starvation
To accept anything for his hunger. She left him,
Returned with a small cup; he looked down into it,
Free of expression, unreadable in a ritual
Of passage years beyond control had created.
She left him with a word of happiness
—Surreal in all this—
As his fingers dipped down into the food,
Completing the ceremony.

September 19, 2025

48. Feline

The boy with the cat on his shoulder
Took exodus with his family along the sea.
On one side the sun was setting with its loveliness,
So apart from this world;
On the other side, the ruins of genocide.
The boy looked ahead; the cat on his shoulder,
Looked back, at the path already tread.
How do these creatures survive in this horror?
And take displacement so calmly?
Every life, the cat, the boy, the family—
How could any of them have survived this?
They moved on, survivors, as the sun
Made the day's end livid and then offered up
The stars. The family didn't rest. The cat
Once started, at the insistence of a distant drone,
Its night seeing eyes flickered with worry.
The boy shot up a hand, to keep him still.
The cat accepted, but kept its instincts aware.
Its eyes knew darkness better than the creatures
Who bore it through this madness.

September 19, 2025

49. Amputees

As he had slept in the tent, a bomb
Had destroyed the boy's leg.
He can't remember now the fury of pain.
They brought him a new leg science had carved.
He smiled. *I can play football with my friends.*
In another tent, a child maybe four,
Rolls a ball around with the stumps of arms.
He too doesn't remember that catastrophe.
His mother looks down at the son
Who will grow into a different life now.
The adults, too: a man on crutches
With one foot of metal, moves with the train
Of the displaced along the sea.
He's not thinking of that old cry—
From the River to the Sea. The blood
Of the occupation has washed him to this sea.

In the years that will come, what will
The bearers of amputations consider,
Their bodies insisting on the fact
Of the evil done? Move away from
The ravaged minds that so violated them?
Or will a quiet revenge be worked?
Will the limbs that science created
Be the flailing of another war?

September 20, 2025

50. The Shudder That Passes

That shudder that passes over a child's face
At the far-off bombs, that jolt of expression
Tumbled like a current whose full flow they know
Without really knowing why, running
To a mother with a gurgled cry;
After the sounds, the explosions elsewhere—
But they feel them beneath the small legs—
The terror remains like an echo
No smiles later will silence or drown.
You look in these faces which in other moments
Seem calm, the eyes that see the things
Of their few years, but the wash of fear,
Its abrupt, definite waves, swirled in the coves
And bays of the heart, leave something
On the deserts of the soul of a child
That no words later, no comforts
Will efface—and certainly not explain.

September 21, 2025

51. *Cries Within*

A moment ago, a building: now it's rubble.
They rushed to this tragedy—and it was:
The cries of many, trapped inside. Cries, screams.
The men began to tug at the debris, praying, cursing.
Some of it came away, but only some;
They were defeated by the mass of destruction.
Inside the voices continued: among moans
And screams were now names—assertions of being.
As if telling those outside who could not save them
To carry away the fact of their death.
The helpless rescuers, who still persisted,
Their hands scarred with blood and dust,
Would pause for a moment, making sure they heard,
Understood, remembered the name of a life,
And called back; they would be the witnesses
Who carried the names of the dead.
Hours later, a day later, the cries had stopped.
The men still pushed flesh against stone.
Perhaps, before another bomb came,
They would reveal even one of those
Who had passed down another name of the murdered.

September 21, 2025

52. Exodus

The long line of people heading south along the sea.
The murmur of their steps and voices.
The sun setting westward, somber with color,
A ruptured slash of red across its disc.
Something old in this; something of our future.
The cars and trucks piled ridiculously high,
Precarious possessions chosen in haste and fear.
The old and injured on wheel chairs,
Children with younger siblings on their shoulders;
For so long they've had to bear burdens of love.
Thousands and thousands are still in the city:
Some will come this way soon; others vow
To meet death on their land. Their bodies
May or may not be found in the rubble.
With night the sun falls into the sea,
And the stars that border summer and fall
Show themselves in this sky. Oh yes,
The star naming people, who now wearily escape
Beneath the celestial they named.
The headlights cannot drown all of heaven—
And suddenly flashes the silhouette of a woman,
Bent with hunger and exhaustion, falling
Without sound in the midst of the caravan.
Vehicles stop; she is raised, taken in
By one of the cars. The stars and the headlights
Continue their contrast of Earth and this passage
Of a people marked for death, but some of whom will live.

September 22, 202

53. *Every Life Here Is Resistance*

The decapitated woman held within her a child;
A child the doctors and nurses brought into this life.
Enwombed all its existence through the genocide,
Feeling in the blood of its mother the fear alongside love,
Feeling through that flesh the explosions,
Moving irrevocably to that arrival of birth,
Then come into this world to a dead, faceless mother.
Oh, there are thousands of marked children here,
But this one…. He or she will bear this hard story,
This fierce story, of the mother's fullest sacrifice,
Of the doctors and nurses who brought this infant life
Into the resistance of life. For every life here is resistance;
Every fact of being is denial of the occupation.
Every breath rebels against death. And the child,
Knowing its history, will not forgive, and will proclaim.

September 13, 2025

54. The Masses

From above, the big, long aid trucks moved
Toward a dark mass—that parted.
And a dark, swarming mass gathered behind.
Then you saw the running men, in places distinct,
But most embroiled in the mass that surrounded
The trucks. What sad, desperate instinct energy
Now engulfs and even climbs the trucks;
You thought of dark ants over a sliver of food.
But these running men, these climbing men
(And a little closer you could hear their shouts and cries)
Could not devour their needs right there:
They were charged to return, return with something;
And even as the trucks were engulfed, many
Were running off with flour and lentils
And even a treasure they could feast on
As they returned across the wasteland,
Often through scattered gunfire,
Often to find one of the family dead—or all;
And they would burst through the shrieking
Of sudden mourners, and fling down
The mockery of the sustenance they'd carried
And surrender to an exhaustion that was beyond
The flesh and fit for this madness—
And in stupor return to what seem like old memories
Of swarming by the aid trucks, reaching, shouting
With hopes that would completely prove delusion.

September 25, 2025

55. Through Israeli Eyes

They seem incomprehensible to us now,
These others, whose bodies move and threaten
On the other side of borders, in towns we surround
With soldiers. What were they to our grandparents,
Our great grandparents, who came from Europe
With wounds and fears and plans of further war
Disguised within salvation? What were they in that clash
And the displacement we configured,
Hailing their departure as the purpose of divine story
In that land whose people we are now?
The old Cannanites peering, arisen from the slaughter
Our one God commanded? Oh, we gave them so much to *be*.
Now their presence exhausts us through generations,
A presence that seems endless. No matter the blood
They gave us in both pain and mockery,
The bodies broken, their children killed in the thousands
But yet are born; even in this war we see they are seeds.
It's their survival we can't comprehend, even as
We declare our own. It is as if the mountain of their loss
Ensured the most terrible victory, as if corpses
Were still alive, and fought us and in whose eyes
Some of the more mad of our own saw demons.
We didn't understand we too were incomprehensible.

September 26, 2025

56. The Speech

What did Netanyahu think and feel as he faced
The emptied chairs at the UN? Of course,
The disguise of his soul mocked them;
The words he gave the scattered remaining
Would be no less righteous. He held some list
Of the barbarism of the Arabs to the West,
But gave no accounting of the larger clash
The latter had wreaked—to Bibi's pleasure.
But did he feel now that the few who would receive him
Had narrowed his course into crosshairs in which he
Might be victim? He must have flashed some reassurance
Of the past through his fierce inner visions:
The standing ovations of the US Congress,
The tired obedience of his troops meeting him
In the wasteland they'd plowed, while some corpse
Tousled in an abstract of rubble lined the frame
Of such memories. (Did he ever consider these corpses
Had known of him?) But maybe some static fragmented
These visions, interruptions, like that of the chaos
Of the protesters outside, defaming him,
And the somber reports titled: "Genocide"—
The survivors of Holocaust now reflection of that horror.
He pushed himself back, to justifications of Yahweh
Commanding destruction of the worshippers of other gods.
But wasn't he one of those idols now, fallen in suicide
Through the violence he believed allowed?
Until the job is finished, he boomed.
And left the assembly believing the dead

That accompanied him necessary payment for the labor
Of the fulfillment of the most divine cruelty
Decreed in the land the invaders had imprisoned.
September 27, 2025

57. *Final Resting Place?*

The final displacement—or would it be the last?—
The family's tent stretched out on a landfill
Of barely covered garbage. The war, of course
Had created other debris, not just of buildings,
But shredded bloodied clothes once filled
With bodies that were now past all this.
There's nothing here now to bomb, the father said;
But the mother felt exposed. Two children,
Five and two, the last born just before the genocide,
Would stumble over the wasted landscape,
The older helping the younger not to fall;
And pointed at the body of a dog long rotted
Past the realm of stench. The mother's call
Was to return to the tent. But whether beneath
That slim roof or the open, death could easily come
At the whim of some drone. So the family lived,
Waiting, hungry, fear dulled to the resignation
That only chance granted tomorrow.
The father wouldn't look at what was past tomorrow;
And the mother lamented: *What will it be for them?*

This was more the father's fear than anything.
So many had died now for the land—whose stretch
He saw was refuse and the violation of the bombs.
One night he dreamt the question: *Where did the flies go*
When the dead dog no longer fed them?

September 28, 2025

58. Tents

They had to patch the tents with their clothes;
The tents had been so long used, put up,
Taken down, moved in cars, on human backs,
By donkeys, fabric meeting the weather of awful months,
The rips and holes became abstract template
Of tapestry with the clothes that had equally suffered.
A part of a shirt, a torn hijab, coalesced into the tents.
It was an art of emergency. And those who patched
And wove in knew the worth of each suffered cloth:
That shirt's too thin; fold it. This jacket's thick—good.
Some tents became more war-battered clothing
Than tent: as if the shelter the displaced bodies bore
Was a garment hardly beyond their flesh,
Was now this greater, patched room of self that kept them
Only centimeters from the sky and bent in
With convulsion at the winds of the bombs.
The most fragile holy place—because all that lends to life

Is holy. One man, grey and black beard dirty
With the war that had folded years into weeks,
Bent in fits into the mysticism of his faith,
Declared that in days to come, *Tents will be made*
Of our flesh, the skeleton of the tents our bones—
And shelter what is no longer alive to shelter.
He flashed eyes at them that saw past the sky.
The others excused his madness, but sighed at its truth.
September 29, 2025

59. No Escape (From Hearing It)

So the IOF lined Gaza with loudspeakers
On trucks to broadcast Bibi's rants at the UN.
How bizarre for the besieged who heard this,
Demon sounds filtered through the bombs and rifles,
The automaton machines that exploded earth and homes.
Words, exhortations, lies and mad visions
That were one with the weapons that seared and killed.
Genocide play by play, Talmudic blessing, newsreel homage,
Jabbering incoherencies as children exploded
And mothers and fathers were wrapped in white
And carried like sorrowed offering in ravaged streets.

And they caught here and there full phrases—
About a job being finished, a job been done…
As if to slay them all were a disciplined labor.
If the words of that voice, woven into
The minutes of horror that were eternal,
Could be stripped from what eye beheld and flesh knew,
Could be spoken without its army of destruction—
What indeed would be the soul of this man who declared
Destruction and triumph, love of war unending?
Naked without the powers others allowed him?

September 29, 2025

60. The Dog in the Caravan

The small dog was happy atop the piled mattresses
Of the caravan of the displaced—part of the pack,
Moving through day's light tumbled with chaotic hours.
The dog's long dirty hair was matted like an armor;
A flap sometimes hung over his eyes a bit.
But he saw, he was happy. He did cringe, even cry out
At the sudden ugly sounds of war. He looked about
As if for escape, or at least consolation.
Then after some quiet, and the caravan moving,
He seemed to lose that terror. Like a child's smile,
Wiped away by the bombs, finally returning.
But, like the children, certainly each moment
Of death being just at the perimeter—or crossing it—
Must stay somewhere behind every returning smile.
And one could read in a dog's bark
A reservoir of the threat of the bombs.
If this ends, and the dog is groomed and clean,
And he and the displaced have homes,
Will this eruption of cruelty stricken through
The shining dark eyes look about the present
Ever caught in the forces of yesterday?

September 30, 2025

61. News Report

The child who could not have more than five
Described like a reporter how his parents had been killed
Right before him. *They came when were asleep.*
They shot my father and my mother.
She was pregnant again.
He stopped, as if expecting the question:
In front of you? It was of course, rhetorical,
But the one who questioned needed to be sure
The horror he was given could not be denied.
–*Yes.* The child, nodded, giving the last fact.
But what unfathomable seeing was in those eyes?

What child can be so numbed to death,
To his family rendered before the youngest seeing?
The children playing, even laughing in the breaks
Of the violence—they bear, they carry the scenes
Of barbarity that touched so closely their blood,
The barbarity that was rendered because of their blood—
Will they survive with the template of fated murder?
Or will they accept their only survival is to resist?

October 1, 2025

62. Birth

It might have seemed a ritual to someone dropped in
From another world, the doctors and nurses
Gathered in a ravaged hospital for a birth,
But the mother was decapitated and baby still alive—
And so they pulled from the newly dead new life,
Heard its cry of earthly affirmation.
They had become expert in every form of bizarre suffering.
But a nurse, beard grey with the war, who had grown up
In these now vanished streets of Gaza, muttered, *Even this*.
The doctor, a mother herself with one child killed,
Said to herself, *Where's the head?* She imagined
Skull and flesh ripped in rubble, the mother's dead eyes
That could now not see what her body had carried.
So the doctor, in reverence, held up
The baby to the headless body as if it could yet witness
Her child. Then all bowed, reverence here too,
As if they had answered, in their own weariness,
All that could be asked of them. And the child
Was brought to the motherless machines
That might keep it alive if the power didn't fail
Or other bombs came—if the soldiers themselves
Didn't come to cement their destruction.
What more potent mark of this time could this child bear?

October 3, 2025

63. *The Day's Catch*

Distracted by the Sumud Flotilla,
The occupation did not keep the people
From the sea. Starved, they sought the bodies
Living beneath that moving sun-glistened brightness.
Nets long unused were flung into the water
With great cries, and with great cries drawn out.
On the sands were straining, flipping bodies,
Belly white in day, dying in the warm air.
So the oppressed feed off the innocent.
Inland beyond the beaches, the bombs continued.
Elsewhere, those captured from the Flotilla,
Who had also moved with the waters,
Were imprisoned, fed upon in another way.

October 4, 2025

64. Buzzing Sound

It was before the genocide. The western reporter
Frowned at the drones buzzing over Gaza.
Zanana, a young man told him. *They watch us.*
The reporter had seen many now, and followed
The passage of the drone over buildings,
Their shadows threatening birds of dystopia,
Disappearing in the direction of the occupiers.
I grew up with them, the youth said.
There was contempt and resignation,
Captive to aerial eyes so much a fact
It had stepped aside anger in his soul.

Years later, deep within the genocide,
The reporter crowded the borders of Gaza
As much as he could and saw the black machines,
Unnatural creations of the air,
Slowly moving over their victims.
So many bodies chosen, he thought. *Mapped.*
He had seen by now the videos of the zanana
Over the ruined cities, and even one mocking soul
Making the buzzing into a song—a cry of defiance
From those who held the ground. It came back to him
More than once, the youth saying, *I grew up with them.*

Then one night, in safety by another country's border
The video of that young man now dirty with the beard of war,
Inside some ravaged room by a window at a height

Rare at this stage of devastation; the zanana came close
To glass half cracked away, face and machine
In dangerous proximity, the man (he was that now, not young)
Bellowing something more than resignation
At the thing that hunted him down. Then:
Nothing more to see. The abruptness
Was a particular horror. Had it ended with death,
Or stalemate? The reporter, shaken,
Struck with the thing you can't shake off,
Stayed silent in the dark, returned to the words,
I grew up with them.

After a while, he imagined the eyes that guided
These spies and hunters, registering for further murder
The dark forms that moved about the city,
As if noting the creatures of a fleshless game.
Would those eyes have been upended
By the defiant face on the other of the cracked window?

He shook his head, to shake all this death away.
To grow up with them, but not to end with them.
No, he just whispered softly to himself. *No*....
October 5, 2025

65. Not Old Enough to Live

The list of the children who died in Gaza,
The long list, pages, a thick book,
Carried and read at protests,
Child's clothes spread across a beach, touching
The reach of waves. And their ages at death:
Three, two years; one. Less. The stories
Of fathers who still held certificates of birth
As they collected certificates of death.
Children who knew the mother only days,
Only hours. What memories does that soul
Take from this Earth? What history brought to God?
Children killed before old enough to wear shoes.

October 6, 2025

66. Born October 7

He was a child born October 7.
He was their first child. His life began with genocide.
He had the darkest eyes. Dark like a sanctuary.
He tilted his head slightly, as if with a question.
The parents didn't think then
His birth would be a marker for this horror.
Months later, as they feared for each other,
Feared for the child, husband and wife understood
The impossible grace of the boy, still alive, growing
In the madness that wore at them. Did it wear at him?

He might have known the blasting bombs, tents aflame,
He might have known no walls but the tents,
The long pilgrimages of displacement with no destination—
He might have known all these things
As common to all days here.
Life is this. The strange metal insect things in the sky, droning,
Searching in their heartless hunger.
Grimly one night, beset with dreams, the father said,
What will he think when it's over?
The mother thought to herself, *Will he be alive when it's over?*
And added, *If he has to lose arms, legs, it's better to die.*
Then clutched herself and cried. To lose her son—
Her husband held her; she did not voice her thoughts.
She became pregnant again. One night an explosion,
A fire, displacement again. She lost the child on the road.
Her son, still so young, looked at his mother quietly,
With the dark eyes that had held his privacies at birth.
He's not afraid, she thought.
Just so wounded it's normal for him.
Months later, just before her son was two, she met
A girl also born on that terrible day. Her parents spoke
About the children being marked. *They will live*, they said.
But it was a faith that frightened her. To be born
On this border was too much of a mark.
She told her husband. He shrugged.
Every day everyone is born is the border
That leaves the past...pushes us—into something.
For some reason she wept at that.
They held each other, still, still alive.

Their child had given them a border
That forced passage into the next day and the next.
October 8, 2025

67. *Last Words*
As the days came on and on and the living
Were scattered like flower petals ripped down
From root and sky, last words gathered:
—*My sons told me to wait by the tent. They never returned.*
—*My son told me this world is nothing. There is nothing*
To cry over. It all means nothing.
—*My husband told me to take care of the children*
If I don't come back. —*My brother told me*
To care for his wife. She was four months pregnant.
And then some even prepared last words with purpose,
Before they were needed. Children wrote wills in crayons
In coloring books, as if telling a story.
Give my toys to my sister. She will be happy.
Some knew death would find them speechless;
It was necessary to declare the soul beforehand.
–*To die here is better. To stay, not get tired with leaving.*
—*My children will live to see no bombs in the clouds.*
—*The sea will be ours again.*

And spoke other things afterwards.
But made those assertions their remembrance.
The last words of thousands and thousands:
Oh, this book, pages scattered everywhere, fallen petals,
Once lives of essence, now essence of words.

October 9, 2025

68. *Waiting For Ceasefire*

A clear sky in light's last hour, maybe one small cloud.
(Under a sky like this somewhere people sit at outdoor cafes.)
Children skate past bomb blasted buildings,
Silhouettes past blocky skeletons.
Happy cries seem apart from two years of horror.
Somewhere men mull and agree over the fate of all this.
Are they part of a child's movement, part of this sky?
One child sways, falls, gets up—another child laughs.
The adults have the relief of hope, and smile.

Elsewhere, another child has been killed.
This world has been sated with mourning—
So not everyone knows this yet; only the family

Will have that anguish: if he had only been
In another place for those moments….
If all the dead, in this long-suffering land
Had lived in other moments—perhaps a future
In which they will not be cast as the displaced,
To be moved and battered by the demon visions
Of the borders of the occupation's maps.
Was it all for cartography—your blood mapped here,
Another's there? Beneath, of course, the same sky.

October 9, 2025

69. The Second Return

Only days ago they had taken this road
Along the sea, southward, homes piled on cars
And backs, ruined country on one side,
The waters somber on the other.
Now they headed back northward,
The ruins a past they could overcome,
The sea bright with end of summer glittering.
They had done this before, in the last ceasefire—
To find something left, not everything gone.
But now most of it would be rubble.
Yet they believed they had reclaimed their land.
A relief, a happiness filled them.
No child would be killed tomorrow.

Though no return releases anyone from memory.
A man crouched by a doorway jumbled with debris,
Head in his hands; he cried quietly.
His father had been killed here,
The house brought down with him.
The son of the weeping son saw his father's sorrow,
Repeated mumbled acceptance to Allah—
But his own tears had more sound:
The young cannot bear wounds so silently.
He was more wracked by his father's sorrow
Than his own. Here was a people who mourned
Losses greater than those of their own hearts.

October 10, 2025

70. *Archaeologists*

It's a strange kind of archaeology
To uncover bodies so recently dead
In the wasteland of streets and homes
That were so sharp in photographs
From only two years ago. You could set
These corpses—some shattered bone with flesh
Like ripped old clothes, some just in motion yesterday—
Set them in those photographed streets and know
Poignantly this culture almost destroyed.
For the archaeologists here were of the people
This recent time brought down;
They had uncovered their own civilization;
And they could weigh the dead against themselves,
And see themselves within that wasteland
—Or above it, moving in this sad, sad light.

October 11, 2025

71. *A Butterfly in Gaza*

Is there anything more delicate
Than a butterfly in Gaza?
The girl in her small garden
Would take sudden pleasure
At a butterfly rising from a flower.
When the bombs came too close and the family fled
She looked and looked among now ravaged gardens
For butterflies, but saw none.
She told her family, *When there are*
No more bombs the butterflies will come.
She had the child's gift of marking peace.
One night in the tent she dreamt of a big garden
And thousands of butterflies on flowers.
And she ran into this flurry of sweet creatures—
Then there were so many bombs
And butterfly wings were shattered like glass;
And someone was carrying her
Wrapped in a shroud of membrane-sparkled wings
And she shouted and shouted, *I am not dead!*—
But even awake she did not believe herself.

October 12, 2025

72. Declarations

There comes an hour when the declarations of leaders
Are so hollow you are past anger now.
Anger will come again tomorrow, but here,
Listen to these words whose multitudes of believers
Should have surely scattered in self destruction
With the events we have all lived. Each of the dead
Belies every word here; how the dead were killed
Defames the mad faith we are retold.
There can be no resurrection of the story
That set the tales that began here. The spears
Of the words "bravery" and "barbarism"
Mock true definition, given to the wrong actors
In the play they insist upon writing—the audience
Upon which they insist. But that old script
Has become knowledge for other words,
Another path that will lead us past here.
The amphitheater of delusion and murder
Will be behind us in a valley, darkening
Before the rest of the land, as a sun sets—
Whose rising will give us a truer governance.
For the journey will continue, and will be recalled
With words that will forever shed those lies.

October 14, 2025

73. *You Can Die in the Future in Gaza*
(For Saleh Al Jafarawi and Rasha)

You can die in the future in Gaza.
The young make videos: *If you see this*
I am martyred. And they smile,
And their voices are kind.
Always pray for me with mercy
And make charity in my name.
And they call their graces to parents
And siblings, nephews and nieces.
I wish I had stayed to be your uncle,
But I am sorry, my dear ones.
And to everyone who may resist:
Thank you for standing with us.
We tried to describe our voices in all ways.
I left everything and chose the path that leads to peace.
And even the younger, mere children,
Write to gift anything left in displacement
To sisters and brothers. With little drawings
Of toys, pages with stars on the edges.
I hope my clothes will be given to those in need.
My bead kits should go to Ahmed and Rahaf.
So young to know the end. In the hand of children
The messages, to those who will be left—
Or who may join them before enjoying
These inheritances of love. A ten-year-old girl,
Buried with brother Ahmed, half their faces gone.
And yet no testimony, or will, mentions betrayal.

October 17, 2025

74. *The Dead Prisoner*

They peered over the dead prisoner, just released.
They had seen enough bodies to not be surprised
At this one; yet here, in this poor man,
Was every aspect of the occupation's torture.
The body appeared burnt with death, blackened;
The eyes were blindfolded, the hands tied;
And there was a rope around his neck, corded
Into his flesh as if it had become his sinew.
The occupation had signed this deed,
And did not care who read it.

They freed the hands, carefully cut the noose—
Though some flesh came away. The eyes were last.
Certainly they feared most his eyes.
Closed in acceptance, grief, agony, every energy
Of violation, they could not look back at those
Who had rescued this corpse—which would be nameless.
Likely his only crime to reach this awful end
Was existing as the oppressed. They stepped back,
Covered him with a reverence his final days had lacked,
Each of them silent, considering themselves,
But for a random moment here or there,
Expired so brutally into anonymity,
The sightless afflicted face become visage
Of a people who knew suffering was not choice
But the cruelest gift of being.

October 18, 2025

75. *Bloody Child(ren)*

A child, bloody, slashed with cuts
—Could flesh be so shredded and still be flesh?—
Alive but numb, breathing slowly,
Blood a half mask on the face.
A child that has drawn everything
Into the self to just breathe,
The one strength left, the focus.
And you remember the occupation's leaders
Saying no child can be left in Gaza.
So the first time you saw a child like that
You understood. And after seeing many children,
Bloody and bomb tossed, with the half masks of blood,
Many not breathing at all,
The words of that evil exhortation become
Accepted threat—become explanation.
You don't even wonder if one who spoke thus
Could behold child after child, sputtering breaths and blood,
Or dead and bloody, perhaps a limb blown away,
You don't even wonder if it would stay their hearts—
Because, you think, it would be, to them, fulfillment.

October 19, 2025

76. Musicians

Four musicians with guitars, on the sands,
By the tents whose flaps rise with seas winds,
The tents that swell with worn shelter,
It's too lovely: the music, the way they embrace it,
At rest now, after the longest journey,
The sky with cloud islands, the waters beyond,
Birds in some safe, safe distance.
It as if all this were ample protection for
Anything they've suffered, anything that will come.
And the other tents along the sea are audience
From where figures emerge, small and moving,
And who pause to capture some of this beauty,
Remain with it, heal in its essence,
So pure, it is past defiance.

October 21, 2025

77. The Libraries of Burning Books

They bombed and burned books as they did bodies.
In one of the first displacements, a boy
Stole into a library that had welcomed his mind
As a child. His heart was stunned
By the collapsed shelves weighted
With seared twisted books and ash.
He took some of the surviving books

With him, not so much to have
But to save, darting out with them as if
Further calamity would return, One was Rumi.
The old poet would console him—
Was that the word?—in the terrible future months:
Wars, like children's fights, are meaningless, pitiless
And contemptible. And so the boy wondered,
As he witnessed the dead borne in carts
Pulled by donkeys, if only the suffering know
Real contempt. The killers must have contempt,
For people and libraries—but, Rumi was right:
It had no meaning. This conquering was absurd.

II

Others would be drawn into the ruined libraries.
For shelter during the worst bombing; and,
Like the boy, for all the memories of what was held
Within simple walls, upon old shelves.
And they too would pick up the books,
Those yet readable, not fully slain, sometimes
Even sit in rubble, reading, as if this was all
Aftermath, not in the midst of continual horror.
And also leave with a book, say, of Said.
A young woman read: *You cannot buy the revolution.*
You cannot make the revolution.
You can only be the revolution.
It is in your spirit, or it is nowhere. This reader promised
Herself she would never allow the revolution
To escape her. Though in later months,

When bravery was called to face every hour,
She considered: *If I die, do I fail the revolution?*

III
The occupation too had occasion to enter
The libraries. One soldier, having just burned
A house, came into a library perhaps out of urge
For further conflagration. But there was already
A quiet fire burning in a corner, spines and pages
Being consumed. *I'm not needed*, he laughed to himself.
And he sat, not far from the flames. It was cold
Outside; here it was warm. Destruction was always warm.
He picked up the books in Arabic, tossed one into flame.
Then discovered some histories in English:
The decline of Rome, the Peloponnesian wars;
The Arabs against the Ottomans. The soldier
Had grown up in America; he could read this;
But it was too much history to consider
Amidst forays of plunder. But no plunder here;
He took nothing. He did not consider he carried out wars
That would be woven tightly into near histories.
He tossed the Peloponnesian wars into the fire
And walked back out onto the bombed streets,
Greeted companions with a great happy cry,
Glad to escape the library of burning books.

IV
And so much later, a member of his family dead,
Moving and escaping death constantly,

The boy who still carried Rumi, read painfully:
Inside this new love, die.
Your way begins on the other side.
He often recited this to himself, like a chant.
The boy passed other ruined libraries.
He felt he did not need to enter them.
He carried enough words to caption the flesh
Slain in this journey.

October 21, 2025

78. Artifacts

When first displaced they took what was needed to survive:
Blankets, clothes, pots. Displaced again and again,
Necessities proved themselves for life.
Now, returning home, to homes utterly ruined,
They sifted through ash and blocks and splinters of rubble
For what had not been essential for flight: photos,
Plates handed down from before the Nakba,
And the toys of children. And so the displaced
Carried these treasures to new homes: tent cities
Far from the cities that once stood;
And between these frail walls recognized
What had once been abandoned and now regrasped
Was what had held them to the violated land.
Sheltering these incessant artifacts
Was what was needed for survival now.

October 22, 2025

79. Inmate

The boy threw stones at a tank.
He was threat to more than a tank; soldiers were at his door.
His mother wept wretched sounds;
His father's face was silent fury.
He clutched at his son with a strength
The boy felt would break him.

In prison he knew the evil faces of the guards risen up
Like specters in a tomb. They pushed him with hands
That were not the strength of his father—
There was no protection there.

He heard the bombs of war—he thought.
The guards laughed at his shudder.
You hear nothing; it's too far.
He was kicked and left with some food.

The others prayed as children, bowing to Mecca.
But in that direction was a dark wall.
The boy bowed and prayed to a barred window of light.
The others tried to correct him.

No, it's that way, he said. *The light is more*, he said.
So even his own scorned him. He lived,
Trying to keep near that bar of light.

Eventually freed, out of indifference or absurdity,
He emerged not a man but a child of wars fought within,

His father dead, his mother much older.

And her tears seemed mutated apart from joyful.
No one asked how he had survived. If they had,
He would have said, *I kept the light upon me*
As I prayed. It's what I have left.
October 22, 2025

80. Cemetery
Look at the land now. A grey powder cemetery
To every horizon, it seemed.
The bodies here have no markers of stones,
No names, no years. wrenched from every marker
Of earth and time. Those who rescue the dead
Bring them up: dozens, a hundred, hundreds,
Bodies with faces crushed in the collapse of homes.
In the light of the day that will not resurrect them,
They are the figures of the future destroyed.
White shroud after white shroud will cover them.
Placed in rows—as if each one was reminder
Of the one before it, the one after;
Mourned en masse by those who will continue
To bring more souls to the white shrouds.
Will there ever be a last, final body?
Will there ever be the conviction that now
The last of the dead are done
And we can rescue the living, the life ahead?
October 23, 2025

81. *Cartography*

Sometimes it was entirely a wasteland,
Flattened rubble and powder
With maybe half a building left in the distance.
There was nothing the eye could say
Was this town, this street.

He walked here because he needed to create
A map of things that would last,
To leave markers for the next people
Of his people to find, to navigate.
With nothing to fix upon, it's a labyrinth.

That struck him; he understood.
You didn't need a maze of walls.
Rip every wall down, leave it rubble
Without the compass of sight—
And no exit remains.

So he broke the maze slowly.
He had the sun to guide him.
And at night, there were stars.
He needed the celestial
To defeat what the earthly had done,

October 25,2025

82. The Future That Killed Them

It was the future they were never allowed
To enter that killed them. The machines
They were never allowed to form
Were in the skies every hour
And the bombs came from the insistence
Of companies around the world
And even in the streets machines
Without drivers exploded at random—
Or design. And the soldiers like invaders
From science fiction, their uniforms armor,
Their faces behind a terrible glass
With no human feeling revealed,
The people of the land just animals
To kill or drive off, the young like nests
Of insects that must not be brought forth.
The movies of the apocalypse
Were brought forth every moment—
Without ever having any life in a past
That could saved them from today.

October 27,2025

83. Artifacts II

A wedding card found in the rubble of a home;
Children's hieroglyphics on a wall;
A tapestry shredded, a curtain slashed
By windows shattered with bombs.
A telescope on a roof, blown apart:
Here's the disc of a lens that saw stars.
A bowl for a cat, a spoon on a clattered floor.
A school notebook with an essay on America.

That stops the one who scavengers:
Is there some illumination in these lines,
Some sight firsthand experiences allows,
For all its blinding? For all the artifacts here
Have been given the random sorrow
Of destruction and recovery by the country
That sent violation to the old world from which
It came, trailing God and dominion.

October, 28, 2025

84. The Child's Hand

Every day he came to the small mountain of rubble,
Knelt down to touch his daughter's hand,
Withering now and drying with death.
So carefully he touched this relic of his life,
And her death. He recalled this tiny hand
Grasped around his thumb after her birth.

–He had not been home then,
Returned to find the world crushed upon her.
Just the hand left, offering to the outside
A child's still reach, open to the sky.
The father waited now for the clearers of debris,
The ragged blocks of thousands of homes.
Soon they would arrive here, raise these tons,
And he could take his daughter's body
For a burial with love. And he left the hand
Each day, promising that end to her end.

They did come; they arrived as he arrived.
He expected to be wrenched by his child's dead body,
But was even more stricken to see the hand
Had been gnawed off by dogs. He looked
And looked down and could hardly believe.

Later he could not recall the moment when
They raised her, wrapped her in the shroud.
Carrying her, he felt her body a jumble
Of crushed things; but it was the missing hand
That made him feel even in death
This bitter life kept her from returning to him.

October 29, 2025

85. A Strong Man

When the genocide began he was a slim youth.
The evil strength that came down upon him
Changed him into seeking some fleshly power.
As the towns and cities became more ravaged.
He used its debris to raise over his head,
And jutting pipes, the frames of doorways, to raise himself;
Like the donkeys he pulled carts of rubble,
Straining his legs. He saw muscle come from his flesh.
In this despairing horror he was grimly pleased.
As the city became more ruined his body was stronger.
He looked at himself in shattered mirrors,
A strong man in bombed-veined glass—as if
In destruction he carried a triumph.

Then food became scarce. The efforts
At sculpting his flesh became a hard
Exchange between his will and the body.
Hunger could claim him in dizzy waves,
Once his grasp slipped from a door frame;
He fell into hard rubble, scraped and bleeding.
He understood that the violence that had urged him
To strength was now claiming him,
The sculpture of himself he had created
Undermined. He recovered from one transformation
To another. Around him were more ruins, more death.
He left the solitary contests of strength
To seek others whose strength was will,
The souls that gathered opposed

To the gymnasium of rubble within which
He had sharpened flesh and would now wield it.
October 31, 2025

86. Reminders

When the family returned to their home
They saw the unexploded bomb
Sliced through the wall: 2,000 pounds,
Lines of serial numbers and USA.
The father touched the initials
Of the land of democracy,
But would not push hard against
The now roughened metal.
The family had no other shelter, they stayed
In another part of the home, balancing
Every day on chance—which had taunted them
Throughout two years…and before.
The bomb remained, like a portrait
No one would go near, or a reflection
Of faces other than these dispossessed
—Monolith of a sky god that needed no features.
What twist of physics held it from its mission?

—While elsewhere, two little twins,
On a ground of fantasy and ruin,
Found an imagined toy that exploded
And ripped apart their lives. They lived,

But bore the attack of the reminders.
Throughout Gaza they were scattered;
And perhaps this *had been* their mission,
Ever the stark inexorable call of their purpose:
We are here still, we can kill you, still.
November 2, 2025

87. It Goes On

Every word of war you know, you lived it
Without speaking, with the days you moved through,
The todays of repeated bombs, the mornings ahead,
Unsure of awakening, the streets of sunlight and dust,
The mad exhausted faces that capture smiles like a mask,
A child waving at life with the stump of an arm,
A call to prayers as if thousands had not been killed,
Just been transferred to other realms promised
And promised to you, too, if one obeyed
What now seems too close and too far,
Your feet almost unable to walk in any direction,
Because in any direction you did walk, again
And again, walk to no destination of safety
Because death could take you anywhere,
For the universe had been ripped open, your flesh
Called for food, rest, not skies of incessant drones
Through which you knew you'd be viewed,
The summation of your days held electrical,
Digital, infrared or coded or blurred or precise,
Image of the unknown of you, target escaped

To life too often—so that now you stumble
Past borders only the drone eyes know,
Feet too exhausted to note any mark
That occupies your people into geography,
The land that you are told, that you believe,
The land that yes, you feel, is the reason you proceed,
A being resurrected without death while you've felt
Month upon month death the closet companion,
A guest so constant you could be rude to its presence
And not feel you increased chances of its consummation
With your days, that continue, on and on,
Day sky and night sky, sun and stars and clouds
And the rains which when they come you remember
Flooded the tents and you were fortunate to sleep on a cot
Above the puddles, or surrendered the cot to another
With no conception of your generosity, and mention
In the wan dawns after that when one of your own
With PRESS across the chest inquired of your troubles,
For you couldn't really speak of yourself, or anyone else,
As all life, your brothers and sisters and children
Had become one action of survival, and the old,
So thin with bone and skin, who remembered
And remembered the passage to this, passage so constant
It seemed stationary, gave weak voiced lament
Or no words at all, just silence under squinting eyes
That appeared to already see the harsh sun
That would come after the clouds, telling you
That if you are not called to something beyond prayer
You will be as they, in a world duplicated, unchanged,

Which does raise some fury in you, if you're still
Strong enough for anger, because as much as this
Is habit and you've fallen into its book
And know the scent of displeasure between every line,
There is something you still hold that batters you
And rescues you from resignation
And you place a hand on the shoulder of the old
As if in benediction of forgiveness of their being so held
And smile softly at the gaze of their question
And speak something that you yourself
Don't understand, as you move on,
Alive, inexplicable, absurd, transcendent.

November 3, 2025

88. Footnotes

So much more; if only they were footnotes
But they're too large: what urges someone
To film setting fires to homes amidst their own laughter
And kick at chairs peeling apart with flames?
Or to explain the video of raping prisoners
As defense, huddled to block security cameras
Then accuse the outraged as traitors,
Undermining the faith of custom?
And the settlers of the occupation killing sheep,
Gouging out the eyes of lambs before their mothers,
Smashing the heads of all the poor beasts
With concrete blocks driven down with arms of veined fury,
Hating the life of any other who would improbably exist,

Shouting in the tongue of their rage divine mandates?
The stern exhortation of the elected no children should be left?
The simple word is the explanation here—the few old letters:
E-V-I-L: the groaned or whispered or hissed explanation,
The name of the old god grasped and grasping here,
That glares with furious jealous eyes at the hopeful lines
Of children, the littles ones who seek to remain,
Drawing in self-absorption and release
The waves of the sea on walls bombs always shatter.
These will be artifact in this place and era:
Seas, tree, birds, families—all taken…and yet,
Somehow immutable, unremovable, steadfast
Not only in the past, but the coming future,
When the evil god of the chosen
Will wither in their own unrighteousness
And scatter in the furies of their own souls,
Self outcast now, and seared to the wasteland
They sought for others.

November 5, 2025

89. Old Books

The books with cracked spines, edges flaking,
Pages still off white at the center, fading to yellow,
And the sketches or even photographs
Of some old, old time; and the thicker pages
With maps, and the towns, thinly written.
Even the spine of the book said: *Palestine.*
But it was just the name of a land then,
No country at all, say the echoes we hear now
In smug accusations. Well, yes, a land—and
The people who knew it through empires
Came to have its name…perhaps simply in response
To the theft of what they had walked upon for centuries.
But alongside boundaries and names are the disjointed
Eras of donkey carts alongside the weapons
Of this century, now violating the map
The olden people walk through; as if in bearing
An ancient right they won't be broken
By such modern slaughter. Those old books,
Spined *Palestine*, could not have foreseen
This slaughter, and this survival.

November 6, 2025

90. *The One Who Rescues the Dead*
After the ceasefire—in which there was still killing—
He was among those who sought the dead in the ruins
Of the destroyed cities, the ravaged land.
Walking alone in the rubble, sometimes he felt
The only man alive in horizons of wasteland.
And the bodies he did see held every recognition
Of something evil having consumed their lives.
Caked with the powder of debris or crushed by chunks
Of buildings or almost wholly burned, or all of these,
He wondered with each of these bodies if there had been
Pain before death or had it been too sudden to know dying;
And if there had been knowing before,
What had been the length of that knowing,
Its width and depth—what had been its awful death?
What level of suffering, what level of enlightenment
Had been endured? Then he stopped himself
At "enlightenment." Pain and fear must have drowned
Everything in that last struggle to exist.
But he wondered if some reached the shards of wisdom
That pierce more than flesh in the end.
—Then he pulled dead children from the rubble
And could not believe in any wisdom before this dying,
Only the evil of the levels he mined,
And which he more and more recognized
Even on the days when he grasped none of the dead,
And sometimes saw dusty cracked reflections
Of himself in the shattered glass of windows—
And, once, in a mirror, split neatly in half;

Even if he pushed the pieces together,
The split in his face went down into his soul.
November 7, 2025

91. *Caged*

There was a vague line that snaked through Gaza,
At first a little more than half of the land,
Then a little more than that. Here and there,
Like callous warnings in a legend, were signs—
Asserting passage beyond this point was death.
The people returning to the ruin prepared for them
Tried to keep a fair distance from the borders....
But there were those with the defiant curiosity
Of the oppressed who paused closely by the signs,
Peering past them, and felt, more than heard
Rifles raised against shoulders, curses shot by those
Eager to reach with more than words.
It was as if there were a beast on the other side,
Breathing heavily behind the bars, just waiting
For anyone to poke a hand through— Then the pain
Of the realization that one was looking *from* the cage,
The hands at one side's could reach through the bars,
Motion at the air of freedom.... But the animate danger
Was on the other side, unpenned. And, yes, breathing.
—Not so much heavily, but in control.
November 8, 2025

92. "Harder to Survive Than Die in Gaza"
(For Bisan Owda)

"It's harder to survive than die in Gaza,"
A thousand people said aloud to anyone
Or no one or just themselves when cold,
When hungry, beset by flies and flood,
At least one member of a family thinking this
As they sat at a poor dinner, a shattered home
Stretched around them, debris their table,
Children looking skyward at the memory of kites,
Too young for the words but feeling them
With a depth to be expressed or buried
Alternately in older years. The men lined up
In the outdoor corridors of the aid pens, some to be shot
As they fled with food, their end proving
This pronouncement of their days. Harder,
Much harder, to survive than die in Gaza
Like some test of faith, passing here, among
So many who died by the violence of chance,
In every direction on the powder-rubbled streets
The knowing that someone, that many
In this double-yeared war died there and there—
And below the ravaged cry, or alongside it,
At once a grasp of this fate, and defiance,
That still, throughout this unraveling,
The people who decried their own hard survival
Had given, within the violation, a purity to their land.

November 10, 2025

93, The Children That Return

The children who return to their homes, now rubble—
The little children, with only shards of memory
Of the walls and floors…perhaps they see these
Remains as just another physical place
In their displacement, another place to point to,
Hear a mother's stories they can't understand—
Of a place, it seems, they've yet to visit.
What's vague in memory will be subsumed by the future.
The family will move on; there's no shelter here.
But will linger, with the bittersweet weight of memories.
A little girl, in the rubbled powdered street of debris,
Makes a curious, even solemn twist of her hand,
Like a spell grasped in the air, a signal (it seems)
To move forward. Her brother, commanded,
Joins her—then their parents call out,
Puzzled, and warning them to stay:
If the children remain a little longer, they will recall.

November 13, 2025

94. Longitude

The row of white wrapped dead bodies
Slashed across Gaza like a line of longitude—
The dead whose names no one knows.
The sun is bright; the white shrouds dazzle, bitterly.
Among the worn tents someone holds memory
Of one who vanished; he or she is here exhumed
From devastation and soon to be covered again
By the poised bulldozer, held in ceremony,
In reverence, sorrow, anger, despair—
That no burial can bury. One looks at
The row of the dead, the skies, the ravaged land
The dark bodies of ascendent birds free between them—
And then a cart pulled by a donkey arrives
With another white wrapped body; and the watchers
Of this grave nudge the line of the dead
A bit closer together, so everyone fits.
And the dirt, and powdered rubble, are poured in.

November 14, 2025

95. Dungeons

The children put in the prisons—
A violation worse than they knew on the streets
And bombed homes. By now their years
Were hardly innocent; and the time
With their jailers made more hard the horror
Of not only the evils the world offered
But suggested, a suffering even beyond
What rose and surrounded them every day.

The rooms of music boomed at intentional levels
To crack the brain and assail flesh,
Bellowed dreams of drowning in sound;
Being thrown against walls, the screaming faces
Of guards that could have never been human—
And then, with time, you saw they were.

To some of the older ones, they would cease torture
And make a glorious offer: *Come to our side.*
Inform, betray. Who knows how many youth
Accepted that, and were returned to the apocalypse
With their own brand of sin; and yet, most children knew
The divide between themselves and the occupiers
Had always been too vast to cross. Refusing,
They were returned to the deafening demon music,
The random beatings. Some would live, outlast,
Be thrust back out, to their wounded people;
And, bearing youth's greatest betrayal,
Wondered upon seeing another who had suffered

In that dungeon if *they* had accepted interior transgressions
To walk again in this imprisoned freedom.
November 15, 2025

96. Deluge

In the tents the puddles are at the tops of shoes
And seep up through the mattresses on the ground.
Outside the grey world beats down; rain for days now.
The world is soaked, bodies are soaked—
If not yet freezing, but the chill
That drains spirit, after all the loss and death
Of month after month. As if Nature had fixed
A season that matched the end of all things:
The world of a people that held to a land
Beset now with deluge: some old myth
Of the arrogant God that drowned
His own creation. But in this myth the evil
Are sheltered, the innocent float to doom—
Or at least are bone-stricken by the raw skies.
Desire here is for something dry: clothes,
A tent…a face without tears. But everything is drenched.
A grandfather shelters two little children on his lap,
He speaks to them old, warm things;
While grandmother, in a puddle, knowing the tent
Is as wet as the skies, cries, weeps, her face
The deluge of all the sorrow of every year
That comes down upon this world, hour after hour.
November 17, 2025

97. Keys

The one who rescues bodies found the key that day
And the weight of it bore through him
More than two of the dead brought up to light
That morning, crushed and faceless.
The key was from a building crushed too,
Rooms of abstract destruction.
It was one of the old keys: he knew them
From the stories and even photos
The elders had kept from their elders,
The key to the houses the occupiers had taken,
Passed down like a talisman some future
Would use for reopening, reentering,
When the invasion would be gone.
He blew dust from it, wiped it with the sweat
Of hands that had uncovered corpses
And let its small dark weight rest in his palm;
And then his fingers closed over it
Like a soft grasp of passion.
He put it in a pocket against his leg
That would move him away
From the tragedy there was no moving from:
Today's genocide, the past's displacement,
The long, long years in between,
While in homes destroyed by the day
The keepsake of a key was evidence
Of both crime and hope—and transmutation
Of a tool of possession and love,
The metaphor for shelter the heart needs.

. . .

He imagined, scattered here, a thousand keys
In these devastated buildings, waiting too for a hand
As silent as the dead who have been forced to release them,
Stoic tools, part of the tragedy and destruction
But would not be reduced to anything other
Than their purpose. And when he showed the others
They each held it in turn, reverent to the artifact
Each had known at least in legend, some in fact,
Recalling the keys held before them as children,
Antiques the mark of a prior world that survived.

He thought, returning to the damp tent that was home now,
He would show the children the key
And imagined the world it foretold,
For the years they would grasp, when all the dead
Would be freed from what had crushed them
And his family would live with doorways again:
The doors of homes that would be consecrated
Without the fears of history, without keys.

November 21, 2025

98. Gathering Firewood

Bothers eight and eleven went out to gather firewood
For their injured father, sent out with the urgent caution
Of their mother's words. Yet they were children;
They wandered over the unmarked Yellow Line.
The occupation saw them as "suspects," as "threats."
—As the military's reports read.
They were struck, from the air, and "removed."

The occupation has killed thousands and thousands
Of children. The insane numbers fall upon us.
What is the despair, the sorrow, the anger,
The madness in all the families of this nation?
Over children returned to them no longer in life?
Or not returned at all: burnt to vapor?
Buried forever in the collapse of a civilization
The occupiers have to deny?

They who proclaim themselves children of Jacob and David,
Their scripture condensed to assertion of the chosen people,
Had given up all morality when they used this disguise
To conquer this land, where years fell away
In horizons of blood. And every urge for years
Is the final conquering through the children—
Who are easily killed now, like a crop for cannibals.
Older, bearing the wounds of their people,
Youth would use the near future to understand
The duty of resistance. The occupiers know without thought
They face a tsunami of reckoning and that if each child

They slay lessens the deluge, they must foresee
That each death of the other is only the sea's retreat
Until the waters return and overwhelm
And they will be drowned by the very sea they denied,
The people they could never replace, never efface.

November 30, 2025

99. The White Thread of Dawn

Each day now, as a white thread became visible
In the first light of dawn, he gave his prayers
To God who would bring him to night. If it were his will.

In a threatened home, then displacement, and again
Displacement, in a tent through which winds made weather
And rains flooded exhausted feet, he prayed,
Seeking refuge for any evil the day could bring.

So many days brought so much evil he wondered
If the refuge he was given to yet live could become evil;
At the end of day he wrestled that despair away:
Forgive me and have mercy upon me.

He passed, in these days and before these nights,
The mosques destroyed by the occupiers
And understood their hubris, insisting their bombs
Could halt the calendars of his prayers.

So the mornings came, and he rose with worship,
Like the habit of an armor every day worn,
His eyes seeking the white thread perceived.

December 6, 2025

100. *Heaven Is Below Your Mother's Feet*
(For Elianne El-Amyouni)

The occupiers came southward from Europe,
And if they swept across the ancient land
With their gangs and jeeps and militias,
There was also the feeling they had descended,
That something incomprehensible had come down
From the skies. Perhaps it was because
They emerged from the horizons, like the hordes
Of century upon century. –Well, the horizon
Did belong to the sky, and so there was
A shadow descended from the same place as the sun.
The old Bedouins, before the war and the flight
What would become the torture of the absurd,
Were stoic in their regard—sun worn ancient mask faces
That saw every horizon fixed with this plague.
They and the olive trees had withstood the Ottomans
And the British and they didn't understand
This savage thing now covering the venerable world
That had given them light and root and memory.
They walked on this land and the occupiers walked here
And the people first of the land recalled old wisdoms:
Heaven is below your mother's feet.
If the mothers who bore them yet moved here….
It was a cry of the heart that was often wordless.
Even prayers did not have words for this.

The occupiers had their cries, but their violence
Was often silent. In the decades that would collapse

Upon each other with soundless evil—
As if something so sure of itself
Did not need any voice of annunciation—
The old world was at once held and was altered:
Like a people keeping the faces of heritage
In a spectacle where others were masked.
Or was it that the true faces *were* beheld, the visages
Of hubris and conquest…and rationale:
God had come, the UN had come—suddenly:
Ancient commands, modern maps.
Although it was never named as one,
A new empire covered Palestine, in blocks
And fragments and webbed stations of control.
The mothers still moved here, dark shawled,
The young mothers with their tight fury and fear
For their newborn; the older, slower ones,
Cautious for their grown children,
Who could now act from their strength and anger.
Was heaven still beneath their feet?
This land checkpointed by conquerors?
Their land tread over and over with the boots
Of the invaders with their weapons?
While the carts that donkeys pulled in strict apocalypse
Moved under these new skies,
Atomic weapons were being built in the bowels
Of the occupier, dark science pushing toward its power,
And men, decades of men, especially young men,
And children were dragged to prisons that became
Helpless colonies of the suppressed clamor of the true people

The colonialists believed were beasts
Needing this cage, away from the tourists
And politicians who lauded this very last
Colonial usurpation. No one knew it was the last.
Africa and Asia were shedding old regimes
That had captured their histories,
But here Europe could wrest one last democracy
Upon the land mothers trod
And make the natives suffer for it.

So Israel was built upon Palestine,
Working this submersion as if the latter
Had only awaited the former
To accept its violent architecture.
The land declared without a people
Were now housed in the larger prisons
That ended with the horizon of the sea.
And the soldiers dragged away the captured sons
From their mothers, the slain childmen,
The mothers who had to return, walking back
To whatever homes and shelters the age had salvaged,
To rooms empty without their children,
Heaven remaining at their feet.

In the worst time since the first time Israel
Drew its borders and blood upon them,
The mothers now knew many slain children—
And husbands and brothers; and the mothers themselves
Fell too, their final blood with the blood of their families:

Less feet to walk upon the persistent grace of heaven,
The weight of the living decreased.
But heaven does not require number; indeed,
Only the faith of one passing here,
And who stays, in the journey of this cemetery land,
This land saying hope remains: because constant passage
Has shown mirror of the shattered forms who thought
They ruled with the God that allowed them sole benediction.
Heaven is below your mother's feet.
The invaders did not understand if they moved
Upon the same land, what was below them was different.
They cast shadows upon this earth, but the forms
Proclaiming themselves, that gestured and killed,
Cast shadows that were not bodies of this earth
But portals through which the flesh died,
Collapsed in its own covenant,
While the bodies of the people of the land
Moved over the shadows and obscured them,
Even when dying and laid upon the earth
Upon which the mothers had granted heaven.

December 13, 2025

101. Elegy/Remembrance

It's a sad elegy, this third winter, Gaza flooded,
The tents flapping in the winds, as if the sky
Insisted this last bit of shelter be torn away.

A woman weeps, standing outside, wringing
Her child's wet clothes, crying out to the world
Faced the other way, her tears and rain all one.

The other night, in another tent, an infant died.
The cold, the rain, the cruel, soaked, drowning world.
A certificate of death for a life who did not yet
Have words to name the prison.

A day later, in the fake ceasefire, the occupiers
Killed six at a wedding. Absolute metaphor:
No love here, no future. For the occupation
Every groom is Hamas, every bride.

The future will come, unraveled from barbarism.
Even the unnamed dead will have voice,
And from the blood here will be streets,
And gardens—and dry rooms.
Above all, there will be remembrance.

December 20, 2025

102. Gravedigger
(For Abu Hatab)

I've buried so many bodies. Thousands.
Me, one man—I'm old now—in these two years.
The ones whose names were told over earth,
The ones they found, unnamed, buried before
I could bury them. Buried one or two, buried
Many alongside each other, the row of shrouds
Just parted by stone. I could not see the dead;
They had become white forms, already
Not part of Earth, but leaving this, for us, here.
I could not see their faces—but I knew them.
I knew in this shroud was perhaps one I'd seen
On these streets, in homes that had welcomed me.
My brothers, my sisters, my children—my people.

My own son, my own brother, I buried.
I'm old, but the dead need more rest than I;
So my lesser need gives them the greater.
But the earth knows me so much now,
More than any sky, these days that look over me.
I know my bed will be ready.
Who will rest me in the earth, when I'm done?

December 24, 2025

JERRY CIMISI writes about events that are historical turning points.
He can be reached at cimisijerry7@gmail.com

www.ingramcontent.com/pod-product-compliance
Lightning Source LLC
LaVergne TN
LVHW091005080826
845145LV00003B/1136